Presented to

_____

On the Occasion of

_____

from

_____

Date

_____

BY THE WATER

A Collection of Prayers for Everyday

ELLYN SANNA

Scripture quotations marked (NLT) are taken from the *Holy Bible,* New Living Translation, copyright ©1996. Used by permission of Tyndale House Publishers, Inc., Wheaton, Illinois 60189, U.S.A. All rights reserved.

Photography Credit: Matthew Davis–49, 50, 90, 108, 109

Scripture quotations are taken from the HOLY BIBLE: NEW INTERNATIONAL VERSION®. NIV®. Copyright © 1973, 1978, 1984 by International Bible Society. Used by permission of Zondervan Publishing House. All rights reserved.

Published by Barbour Publishing, Inc., P. O. Box 719, Uhrichsville, Ohio 44683
http://www.barbourbooks.com

Printed in China.

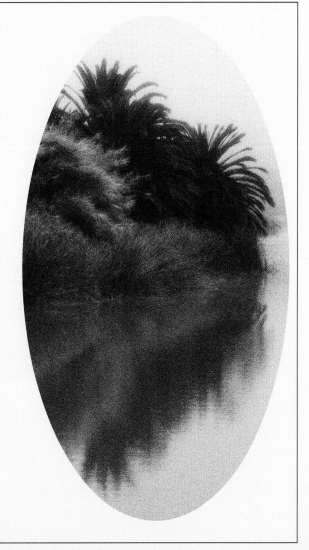

Dedication

May the words of my mouth
and the meditation of my heart
be pleasing in your sight, O LORD,
my Rock and my Redeemer.
Psalm 19:14

Introduction

Through the ages, water has been one of writers' favorite metaphors. The Bible is especially full of water images; Jesus even referred to Himself as living water.

Water means life to us, literally. Our physical bodies, our entire planet, depends on water to live. And water also cleanses. No wonder then that water helps us glimpse God, the one who gives us life and washes away our sin.

But water can be destructive as well. It can flood our homes and farms. It can bring death.

Baptism unites water's two faces, the creative and the destructive. In baptism, our old lives are put to death beneath the water—and we are raised up, clean and pure, to new life in Christ.

Water, then, speaks to us of the gospel. Its constant rippling voice reminds us of eternity, and its ever-changing form tells us of renewal. Water is a signpost that points us to the deeper, eternal world of Jesus Christ.

In college, my favorite song contained these words: "Come to the water, stand by My side"—and back in those busy college years, I formed the habit of seeking God's presence in outdoor places beside the water. I went for long walks up the small, nameless creek behind my dorm, and I spent quiet hours sitting cross-legged on the banks of the Genesee River. Sometimes my heart would be filled with joy, other times my face would be wet with tears, but as I lifted my heart in prayer, God never failed to come to my side.

Today my life is very different, filled with the demands of a family and a career. But I still run away to be with God beside the water, whether it's our little Choconut Creek that flows beside our house or the Atlantic Ocean where we vacation. Through the cycle of the seasons, through all the changes in my life, God always meets me by the water.

From time immemorial men have quenched

their thirst with water without knowing

anything about its chemical constituents.

In like manner we do not need to be instructed

in all the mysteries of doctrine,

but we do need to receive the Living Water

which Jesus Christ will give

us and which alone can satisfy our souls.

Sadhu Sundar Singh

Living Water

From a scientific perspective, I don't really understand water. Oh, I know that two atoms of hydrogen combine with one atom of oxygen to make a single molecule of H_2O. But I can't comprehend what that means, not really. And while I know my body can't live without water, I don't quite understand why.

Theologically speaking, Lord, I don't really understand prayer or grace, either. All I know is this: Spiritually, I can't live without Your living water. And somehow, each time I open my dry heart in prayer, You enable me to drink from Your Spirit.

I don't have to be a scientist to know when I'm thirsty. And I don't need to be a theologian to know I need Your grace.

As the deer pants for streams of water, so my soul pants for you, O God. My soul thirsts for God, for the living God.

Psalm 42:1–2

MY THIRSTY HEART

Sometimes I get confused, Lord. I think that some thing, some person, some place, will fill the emptiness in my heart. It's as though I were thirsting to death—and then tried to quench my terrible thirst with a tall glass of popcorn or a big gulp of mashed potatoes. Popcorn and potatoes are fine in their place—but they will never quench my thirst.

And only You, Lord, can meet the deepest longings of my heart. You give me wonderful gifts, and I delight in them. But my soul is thirsty for You alone. I can never drink in enough of Your presence.

RIVER VALLEY

Over the ages, the Susquehannah River carved a long, wide valley, sheltered on each side by gentle hills. My family and I live in this river valley, the hills at one end of our street, the river at the other. In the summer, we are surrounded by green lawns; in the fall, the trees burn gold and scarlet, while chrysanthemums glow like jewels along the sidewalks. Then winter brings the pure, bright beauty of snow and ice, and the seasons cycle around to spring's new green again.

But some days, Lord, my fears and insecurities press so tight around me, I might as well be living in a gray jail cell instead of a green valley. I'm so afraid that time will rob me of the things I love most that I miss the new gifts each season brings: Mourning over summer, I miss fall's brilliance; regretting that the leaves must fall, I forget to delight in the first snow, and so it goes. The seasons go by me, but shut up tight inside, I miss each month's loveliness, the wealth of life and color that is watered by our river. Your Word tells me, though, that You don't want me to exist in a narrow, fearful space; instead, You long for my life to spread out like our river valley. Throughout the cycle of the seasons, You wait to fill my life with beauty. Sheltered by Your love, Lord, watered by Your living presence, may Your garden spread throughout my life each season of the year.

Like valleys they spread out,
like gardens beside a river. . .
Numbers 24:6

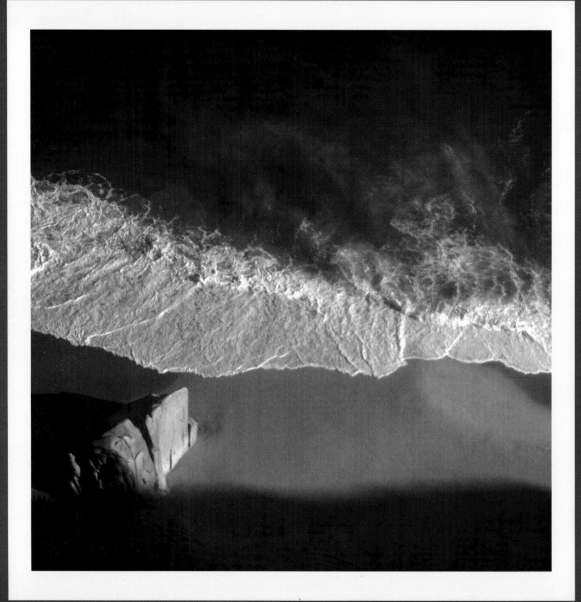

Summer

During the summer months, our family spends many days beside the water, dabbling our feet in the creek, lying on the banks of the river, vacationing at the ocean or by our favorite Adirondack lake. Nature overflows with lovely green growth, and my children and I, freed from the school year's restrictions, treasure our long days together. Summer is a time of great blessing, filled with moments when I sense God's presence with me.

But summer can also be a time of drought. Just as the earth cannot grow and be fruitful without water, my life too will wither and die without God's presence. . . .

My Heart's
Eternal Home

Today my children and I lie on our stomachs beside the river, watching the fish flicker through the water.

"Why don't the fish crawl up on the land?" my youngest daughter asks.

"Because," my son answers, "the water's their home. It's their world. It gives them everything they need."

You, Lord, are my home, too. Like Paul said in the Book of Acts, in You I "live, and move, and have my being." You supply me with everything I need to live, not only now but forever. Why would I ever want to leave Your presence?

In water lives the fish,
my spirit in God's hand.

Angelus Silesius (1624–1677)

14

SEA MONSTERS

My children and I love to dangle our legs over the end of the dock, peering down into the water. We can clearly see the small green plants that float beneath the surface, tiny sunlit bubbles caught among their leaves, but as we look deeper, the lake becomes dark and murky. Down in the darkness, we catch the mysterious shadow of something moving, but we cannot make out the shape. My children shiver with delicious horror, imagining sea monsters.

My own heart is the same, Lord: I can see only a little way into the shadowy depths. Thank You, Christ, that You are the Light; You see clearly both my conscious and unconscious self. Reveal to me those things within myself that I need to see. And please, my Lord, heal the monsters that hide deep within my being.

I think of consciousness as a bottomless lake, whose waters seem transparent, yet into which we can clearly see but a little way.

Charles Sanders Peirce

He leads me beside quiet waters.

Psalm 23:2

A QUIET RIVER

Some days, my life is too full of noise. Music is blaring, the kids are shouting, my husband's power tools are snarling as he remodels our basement, and the phone never stops ringing. I just want to escape somewhere quiet, somewhere peaceful and calm.

So today, I've run away to the creek, just for a few minutes. The wind blows softly through the leaves above my head; a chickadee bobs from branch to branch, calling with its small, cheery voice; and at my feet the creek ripples endlessly over the stones. All these quiet sounds wash together into a river of peace that flows into my heart.

I am grateful, Lord, for the tiny tranquil moments You sprinkle through my life. And when I go back to my house, even in the midst of all the noise, may Your peace flow inside my heart in a never-ending river.

For I will pour water on the thirsty land; and streams on the dry ground: I will pour out my Spirit on your offspring, and my blessing on your descendants. They will spring up like grass in a meadow, like poplar trees by flowing streams.

Isaiah 44:3–4

WATERING THE PLANTS

I have a confession to make, Lord: By the middle of July, I'm ready for the end of summer vacation. I love being with my children, You know I do, but our life becomes chaotic without the structure that school provides. All five of us are home all day, and the house is messier and noisier; I long for the quiet moments of solitude I found in the school-day routine, moments that helped me keep my sanity, my sense of Your presence in my life. On these hot summer days, my children need so much from me—and when I end up snapping at them, I feel guilty and inadequate.

Thank You, God, that You are present in my life even now when I am hot and grumpy. And thank You most of all that You have promised to work in my children's lives. They depend on Your grace, not mine. So please—rain down Your blessings on my children. Help them (and me, too, Lord) to grow strong and green even on the hottest summer days.

MINNOWS

We've all run away today, Lord, my children and I, escaping the summer's dry heat by paddling in what's left of our creek. I thought we would find refreshment, as we have on other days, but this time our cross words and hurt feelings have come with us even here. And I have to confess, Lord, that my temperament today is not much better than my children's.

At my feet, though, minnows swim in silent, peaceful swirls through the creek's brown water. The sun catches their sides, making them glint like silver. Unaware of the hot world of air above them, they draw their life from the cool water that is their home. The events along the creek banks (a car rattling over the bridge and down the street, the growl of a minibike's engine, my children's quarreling voices) do not disturb them. Immersed in the creek's ripples, they slip untroubled from sunshine into shadow and out again.

Jesus, let me be like a minnow in the stream of Your grace. Immersed in You, may I be untroubled by the world's harsh sounds. Teach me to flow with the current of Your peace through both joy and sorrow (and through days full of bickering as well as days of laughter). Show me how to make my home in grace's clear water. And no matter how hot and arid my day seems, may I always draw my life from Your living stream.

All creatures need water to live, but only those who are so designed can actually live within it. That is why those who live by grace are like fish, for just as water is a fish's element, so we live and breath grace.

John Bunyan

TIME AWAY

Maybe, Lord, what our family needs more than anything else is to simply leave our house and our responsibilities behind for a little while. But can we find the time and money to pile into our van, and make the long drive to the ocean?

God, remind us that days together on the beach, reading and sleeping and playing, simply enjoying each other's presence, are never wasted. In those days of sun and sand and water, You renew our hearts and tie them tighter to one other. Our responsibilities will wait for us—and when we come home we'll pick them up again more cheerfully, refreshed and strengthened by our time away.

Jesus withdrew himself with his disciples to the sea.

Mark 3:7 KJV

THE KINGDOM OF HEAVEN

Today we watched the fishing boats bring their heavy loads into dock. Inside the black nets, the fish gleamed like silver fruit. "That's a whole lot of fish dinners," my husband said.

Lord, thank You that You caught me in Your kingdom's net. May my life shine with holy fruitfulness; help me to give nourishment to Your Body.

The Kingdom of Heaven is like a fishing net that is thrown into the water and gathers fish of every kind.

Matthew 13:47 NLT

NEW PERSPECTIVE

Somehow, God, beside the ocean, troubles fall into perspective. I wake at dawn, while everyone else is still sleeping, and walk the long beach alone, the cold water splashing over my bare feet. The gray water merges with the hazy sky, and the waves rise and fall, rise and fall, a sound that is as comforting to me as a mother's breathing must be to her baby. I sense Your presence here, Lord, and I let all the complications of our lives drop into Your hands. Best of all, as I surrender my heart to You, You give me Your heart in exchange.

Meanwhile, to the east the gray sky begins to gleam like an opal. As the sun climbs higher, it burns away the mist, leaving behind a world of blue and gold.

I must go down to the seas again, to the lonely sea and the sky. . . And a gray mist on the sea's face and a gray dawn breaking.

John Masefield

CLOTHED WITH LOVE

Lord, sitting here on the sand while my children build castles down by the waves, I am completely, utterly content. The ocean, my old familiar friend, roars and sighs in front of me, its noise as constant as Your love, and out at the horizon, sky and water meet in a long lovely line of blue. At last, my heart is quiet and relaxed, open to Your presence.

Thank You, God, for the wonder and beauty of creation. I am grateful for eyes to see, ears to hear, lungs to breathe, skin to feel. . . . Thank You for clothing everything with such love.

Great wide,
beautiful,
wonderful world,
With the
wonderful water
round you curled,
. . . World, you are
beautifully dressed.

Matthew Browne
(1823–1882)

THE GLORY OF THE LORD

At home, Lord, living so far from the ocean, I forget how great the sea is. But today, from the lighthouse windows, all I could see was endless water stretching out to meet the sky.

Sometimes, I get so busy with my life that I forget who You really are. Remind me again and again, God; cover me with the knowledge of Your endless glory.

for the earth will be filled with the knowledge of the glory of the Lord, as the waters cover the sea.

Habakkuk 2:14

> *The LORD will*
> *guide you always;*
> *he will satisfy*
> *your needs in*
> *a sun-scorched*
> *land. . . you will*
> *be like a*
> *well-watered*
> *garden, like a*
> *spring whose*
> *waters never fail.*
>
> Isaiah 58:11

Now that we've been home again a couple of weeks, how quickly our vacation's refreshment has evaporated from our lives. I feel as hot and cross as I did before, and our lawn is dry and crunchy, an ugly dull brown where only the weeds are green. The river is so low that it looks more like the creek, and the creek has nearly dried up all together. My flowers that were so beautiful earlier, a riot of pink and gold and purple, are skeletons with dry, black heads. And forget about the tomato plants; we won't be having homemade sauce this year. Even the trees' leaves are beginning to turn brown. Everything looks so ugly.

Oh, Lord, my own heart is not much different. This past week has seemed to drain all the moisture from my life. I've kept on going, running back and forth between my parents and my children, trying to be a good daughter and a good mother, trying to meet everyone's needs—but inside, Lord, You know how dry I feel.

But Isaiah guarantees that You will satisfy our souls even in drought times. No matter how long I go without spiritual rain, You promise I will be like a lush, growing garden.

All my rivers have dried up. So I'm looking to You. Please, Lord, water my garden.

Rivers in the Desert

Outside my kitchen window, the dogwood's leaves are beginning to curl yellow and brown from lack of water. And inside my heart, I feel just as dry. My life keeps going, no matter how I feel: My house needs cleaning, my children need my attention, my husband needs my companionship, my parents need my help, my career needs me to devote hours of sleepless nights if I'm ever to catch up with all my work. But how can I continue to work and give to others, when spiritually I am thirsting to death?

My life looks like a desert right now, Lord. Please open up a river inside my dusty heart. Let Your love spring up inside me, so that those around me can drink from the fountain of Your life.

The poor and the needy search for water, but there is none, and their tongues are parched with thirst, But I the LORD will answer them, I, the God of Israel, will not forsake them. I will make rivers flow on barren heights, and springs within the valleys. I will turn the desert into pools of water, and the parched ground into springs.

Isaiah 41:17–18

29

Broken Cisterns

When I worked in a Mexican orphanage, we depended on a cistern for part of our water supply. During the winter months, the cistern filled up with rain water, and the orphanage relied on it during the long dry season that followed. But one summer the cistern cracked, and the precious water ran out into the ground.

This summer, Lord, I've been so busy with my life, running here and there with the kids, meeting friends, driving across the state to visit my parents and my in-laws, keeping up with my professional responsibilities, trying to fit in time with my husband. I've wanted to see myself as strong and independent, able to handle life all by myself, as though I had my own personal store of living water inside me.

But in all the summer's hustle and bustle, Lord, I forgot to spend time with You. I've been acting as though I had a well of life within my own heart—but now, faced suddenly with a family crisis, I realize just how empty my heart is. All my strength has leaked away.

Forgive me, Lord. My heart is a broken cistern that will never hold water for long. I am dependent on You, the never-ending fountain of life. Thank You that Your grace springs up anew for all eternity.

My people have committed two sins; They have forsaken me, the spring of living water, and have dug their own cisterns, broken cisterns that cannot hold water.

Jeremiah 2:13

God will never plant the seed of his life upon the soil of a hard, unbroken spirit. He will only plant the seed where . . .the soil has been watered with tears of repentance.

Alan Redpath

THE RAIN OF REPENTANCE

I've been complaining to anyone who would listen, including You, Lord, about how hard my life has been these past few weeks. I've been overwhelmed with work, my family is in the midst of a health crisis, and this hot weather is sapping all my energy. Something has to change, I keep saying.

Well, something does have to change, but it's not work or my family's health or the weather. It's me. I've been angry with You, God, for not changing the outside world—and meanwhile I've refused to let You alter who I am on the inside. My heart has been as hard and rocky as our garden.

Tonight, though, I've been watering my heart with tears of repentance. Please, Lord, let the moisture sink deep, all the way down to my roots.

O thou Lord of life, send my roots rain.

Gerard Manley Hopkins

He who. . .
calls for the waters
of the sea
and pours them out
over the face of the land—
the LORD is his name.

Amos 9:6

THE LORD

Today at last rain clouds are rolling in over our hot, dry land, carrying water picked up from the Atlantic. Our thirsty land will be refreshed!

Help me, God, to trust Your timing for my life. I surrender myself to Your plan, for You will never fail me. You are the Lord. And You do all things well.

I want that grace that springs from Thee
That quickens all things where it flows;
And makes a wretched thorn like me
Bloom as the myrtle or the rose.

William Cowper

FAITHFUL GRACE

At the beginning of the summer, my husband wanted to cut down that old rose bush in our yard. It was a bunch of tangled thorns that looked as though it were completely dead. "Give it one more chance," I pleaded, and instead of removing it, he pruned it and fertilized it and watered it faithfully. Meanwhile, I forgot about the ugly bush in the corner of our yard—until I looked out today and saw it covered with yellow blooms.

Thank You, God, that You've never given up on me. All through this long, hot summer, You tenderly watered my life with Your grace. I thought that parts of me were as dry and lifeless as those dead, tangled thorns. And now, to my surprise, I find my life has burst into bloom once more.

33

God, I've been wandering in the wilderness, feeling like Hagar—lost, rejected, thirsty, and full of sorrow. But when I turned to You at last, You opened my eyes. Even here, in the midst of my life's troubles, You put a deep well of grace. It was right beside me all along.

Then God opened (Hagar's) eyes and she saw a well of water.

Genesis 21:19

Autumn

Now, when we walk by the river, the water reflects the trees' bright leaves, and the air is filled with the tang of approaching winter. The autumn months bring new challenges to our family, new rewards, and new opportunities to turn to God in prayer. Our family moves in different directions throughout the day, like a river that branches into many tributaries. And I must struggle to accept that God's grace flows with each small stream. . .and in the end, we will all be united into the great ocean of His love.

Bringing Home the Ocean

Every year my sister brings home bags of shells and rounded stones, collected from her trips to Cape Cod and the Outer Banks. Eventually, I suspect her home will look more like a beach than a house. Her favorite bits of flotsam, the ones that seem to miss the wet gleam thrown on them by the waves, she puts in big glass bowls of water here and there around her house. It's her way of bringing the ocean home with her.

Today, Lord, as I sit alone in my peaceful, shining house, my life feels like one of my sister's glass bowls, filled up to the brim with grace. My children are back to school, happy with their new teachers, glad to see their old friends. For the first time in more than two months, my house is clean and orderly. My whole day lies ahead of me, mine to fill up with work and prayer and my own quiet thoughts. And best of all, in six more hours my family will all be back together again, more excited about each other because we've been apart.

Thank You, Lord, for filling my life with such sparkling joy! I am grateful too for all the shiny stones and graceful curving shells that You have dropped into the water of Your grace.

> Were we wise, each taste of mercy would lead us to the ocean of love.
> John Owen

And, Lord, on those days when my house is once again messy, when I feel pressured and overworked, when I miss my children's hands in mine, remind me then that Your grace is deeper than my small bowl. When my life seems like a dry jumbled collection of broken bits of shell and rock, fill it again with the grace that is as wide and deep and endless as the sea.

RENEWAL

This creek was nearly silent this summer, a silty bed of rocks. Now it's noisy and full of life again. The water leaps and gurgles, constantly changing form as it spills from stone to stone, washing away the summer dust.

Lord, may I, like the creek, be renewed. Keep me from being so rigid that I cannot adapt to the demands of new circumstances. And most of all, may I be changed into Your image as I am made new and clean in Christ.

The fluidity of water. . .the way it constantly renews itself. . .reminds us of the possibility, and the need, for change, and cleansing.
Luci Shaw

*The long light
shakes across the lakes
And the wild cataract
leaps in glory.*

Alfred Lord Tennyson

A GLIMPSE OF HEAVEN

Days like today, God, I see Your presence shining everywhere I look. The autumn trees burn gold and red against the deep sky, and the air is clear and crisp. Beside me, a stream tumbles down the hillside in a bright froth of broken water, then cascades in silver ribbons into the lake below. The sun that touches my face so gently sparks like fire wherever it falls on water.

Thank You, Lord, for the bright, glorious freedom of this autumn day. Thank You for a glimpse of heaven.

Just like the first creation, when the Spirit of God moved upon the face

of the waters, putting creation into order and harmony,

making everything work together the way we still see it working today,

even so the new creation. In other words, our regeneration in God is done

by the same hovering Spirit.

John Bunyan

GOD'S CREATING SPIRIT

As I look out at this quiet lake, Lord, I think about Your Holy Spirit brooding over the waters at the beginning of creation. That was the beginning of all I see around me: the bright sky, the gold and scarlet trees, the chipmunks that scurry beside me through the fallen leaves. And yet even in the midst of all this beauty, the earth is getting ready for winter's death; the trees are letting their lovely leaves drop to the ground, just as I too must one day lay my physical body into the earth.

Thank You, God, that death is not the end of the story. Your Spirit still broods over us, and through Christ, each death only leads us to a new and deeper life. Your creation never ends.

Enduring Love

Lately my family seems to be changing too fast. I feel as though I'm standing still on a riverbank while time rushes by me. My baby who only yesterday was snuggling up to me with her thumb in her mouth now says she hates me because I'm too protective; when did she turn into an adolescent? My father who has always been so strong and sure is in the hospital, sick and weak; when did he turn into an old man? I wish I could build a dam across time, make it stand still—or better yet, reverse it, make it flow backward to a place when we were happier.

You created time, God, and I know Your creation is good. But I'm glad that when time surges past me, so fast that my head spins and my heart aches, You are unchanging and eternal. Your love endures forever—and that same love flows steady and the same in the midst of each of life's changes.

The flow
of the river
is ceaseless
and its water
is never the same.
The bubbles
that float in the pools,
now vanishing,
now forming,
are not of long duration:
so in the world....

Kamo no Chomei

God does not let us look to the hills for our help until we have first seen them submerged in the flood.

John Bunyan

My Help Comes from the Lord

God, I've depended on the stability of my family; it's one of the things that gives me security. But I've also taken it for granted. I assumed that we would be immune to the problems that trouble other families.

All that's changed now. Suddenly, our family is flooded with conflict and pain. The things I've counted on most are sinking beneath a muddy tide of anger and hurt feelings. I don't know what to do, I don't know how to fix things. All I can do is look to You, the one who made heaven and earth.

I lift up my eyes to the hills—where does my help come from? My help comes from the Lord, the Maker of heaven and earth.

Psalm 121:1–2

But when he asks, he must believe and not doubt, because he who doubts is like a wave of the sea, blown and tossed by the wind.

James 1:6

WIND-DRIVEN

Staring out our cottage window, Lord, I get dizzy watching the tossing waves. They shift and swell and break, then rise and crest and crash again, endlessly. They are never still, never solid.

My thoughts go back and forth with the same frantic speed. I want You to solve my family's dilemma—but even as I ask for help, I find that my mind has scurried on ahead, plotting and planning, worrying and fretting. One moment I'm convinced I should take a particular approach to work out our problems, and the next I'm positive I should follow an opposite course of action. *Help, Lord!* I pray, and then I let my heart be tossed back and forth by fear.

Lord, calm my wavering thoughts. I don't know the answer to our problems—but You do. So I come to You, my heart at last quiet and open, asking for Your presence in our lives.

As they sailed, he fell asleep. A squall came down on the lake, so that the boat was being swamped, and they were in great danger. The disciples went and woke him, saying, "Master, Master, we're going to drown!" He got up and rebuked the wind and the raging waters; the storm subsided, and all was calm. "Where is your faith?" he asked his disciples.

Luke 8:23–25

STORMS

The water is raging, Lord, the waves tall and capped with white. The wind howls around our cottage and rattles the window panes. Wrapped up in sweaters, we huddle together inside our drafty shelter, looking out at sheets of cold gray rain falling on the heaving ocean. "I'm scared, Mommy," my youngest whimpers.

I'm a little scared, too, Lord, I must confess. I'm used to warm summer days at the beach when the ocean is blue and smiling; I didn't know how different the coast would be in November.

And I'm also scared of the emotional storm our family faces. Our lives that were so happy and blessed look gray and cold now. Will we ever see the sun again? Or will this storm destroy us?

Remind me, Lord, that You rule the wind and the sea—and You control my life's tempests as well.

Suddenly they saw Jesus walking on the water. . . . They were terrified, but he called out to them, "I am here! Don't be afraid."

John 6:19–20 NLT

WALKING ON WATER

The storm is still raging, Lord, the waves crashing higher and higher. Things seem to be getting worse and worse. As I peer into the darkness, I am filled with foreboding.

And then, somehow, in the midst of the wind and waves, I hear Your familiar voice speaking words of love and reassurance. The tempest is just as wild as ever, but I sense You are present, even here, even now. The waves roar and crash. . .and calmly, confidently, You come walking toward us on the water.

By faith the people of Israel went right through the Red Sea as though they were on dry ground.

Hebrews 11:29 NLT

STRAIGHT THROUGH THE WAVES

Lord, troubles continue to roll and swell around us, like huge ocean waves threatening to drown us. I'm scared, God, terrified, in fact.

And then I remember the way You made a path for the Israelites through the Red Sea. Their destruction seemed certain; but You led them to safety. Surrounded by towering walls of water, they walked on dry ground.

So we'll follow You, God, straight through the waves. You won't let us drown.

"God Moves in a Mysterious Way" is a hymn written by a man who was insane. He was tormented by paranoid fantasies and he heard threatening voices speak inside his head. And yet, despite the dark mental storm he endured, the poet affirmed Your presence, Lord.

When my own emotions threaten to overwhelm me, God, remind me that even in the most threatening seas, I can follow Your footsteps across the waves.

God moves in a mysterious way
His wonders to perform;

He plants his footsteps in the sea
And rides upon the storm.

William Cowper (1731–1800)

It's easier to find and glean the bright colors

where the waves are washing the spread of shells

because the whites are whiter and the reds,

pinks, purples, oranges, are more intense.

Perhaps in the same way, crisis, trouble, grief—

the breakers in our lives—

show us up truly for who we are.

Luci Shaw, *Water My Soul*

AFTER THE BREAKERS

At last the storm is over. Walking along the beach this morning, I found huge gray whelks and perfect gleaming sand dollars, a lovely treasure trove spread out across the sand.

Lord, our family has weathered our emotional storm as well. Our hearts feel sore and battered—but as the tide withdraws now, we understand each other better than we did before. In my family's faces I see something sweeter and more lovely than I could have imagined before our crisis, treasures left behind by the storm.

There, beside the tranquil river,
Mirror of the
Savior's face,
Happy hearts
no more to sever,
Sing of glory and of grace.

Robert Lowry (1826–1899)

A HEAVENLY RIVER

The trees are all bare now, their bright leaves stripped from their dark branches. The rusty yellow leaves float on the river's slow waters, and the gray skies hold the promise of snow.

A man our family loves, a man my children call Grandpa Jack, died today. Grandpa Jack was a humble man who lived his faith quietly and matter-of-factly, without ever preaching. He was a farmer who knew the earth's seasons intimately, and when he faced his own death, he got ready for it, just as each autumn he had prepared his farm for winter.

We'll miss Grandpa Jack, Lord. But when I shiver, thinking of winter's frozen, dark days, remind me that on the other side of the cold lies a warm, bright promise: spring. I'm looking forward to the day when my family and I and all the saints and angels—and Grandpa Jack—gather together by the living river that flows from Your eternal throne.

The "water of life" is the Spirit,
the grace of God, and the spirit of life. . . .
The water is better than any mirror,
for here in the clearness of grace,
we have the chance to truly see ourselves.

John Bunyan

IDENTITY CRISIS

Sometimes I avoid mirrors; I don't always like to see myself as I really am. I'd rather wait until I'm dressed up with all my makeup on before I examine my own reflection.

But, Lord, when I lean over Your River of Life, the image I see is clear and sharp. In Your grace, I find my own self revealed. The process is often uncomfortable, sometimes even painful. But as I dare to look deep into those clear waters, I find I'm also seeing You.

As Wide as the Sea

Outside, Lord, the sky is like cold, dull metal. Dead leaves skitter along the road beyond my window, while I huddle shivering inside a quilt, my throat sore and my head aching. Gray November days like today, shut in my house far from the water, it's hard to remember sunshine and warmth and a wide, shining sea.

I'm too sick to go anywhere—but I have a nagging sense that I've let people down by backing out of my responsibilities. I feel guilty and anxious, my thoughts cloudy and fretful.

Thank You, God, that Your kingdom does not rely on my feeble efforts but only on Your grace. I may be shut up in my stuffy house—but the sea is still as wide as ever; its endless motion does not depend on my presence. And here alone, sick with a cold, I may not sense the vital action of Your love—but Your mercy endures as always, limitless and shining.

There's a wideness in God's mercy,
Like the wideness of the sea. . . .

Frederick W. Faber (1814–1863)

My life is like
a broken bowl,
A broken bowl
that cannot hold
One drop of water
for my soul
Or cordial
in the searching cold;
Cast in the fire
the perished thing;
Melt and remould it,
till it be
A royal cup for Him,
my King:
O Jesus, drink of me.

Christina Rossetti

A Cup of Living Water

This morning, Lord, as I hurried around trying to fit in a little housework before the children's breakfast, I found myself dusting that old cracked tea cup again. *What a waste of time,* I couldn't help but think. Why do you suppose I'm so attached to something that's not good for anything except collecting dust?

I put it carefully back in its place, but then it occurred to me: I feel as empty inside as that old cup! You are the Living Water, and I know You want to pour Yourself inside me. I long for You to fill me—but instead, my life is dry and empty, like my cracked tea cup put up on the shelf, no practical good to anyone.

If I'm honest, Lord (though You know how hard that is), I'm as attached to my life as I am to that cup. I want You to fill me—but I want to keep my life just as it is, useless and broken. Oh, I may acknowledge a few hairline cracks, but I carefully keep the rest of my life intact, safe and dusty up on the shelf.

But I'm tired of being empty. Take my life's cup, Lord, and let it smash on the floor. And then start all over. Shape me into a pure, crystal container that brims over with Your Spirit.

Love is a great thing provided it recurs to its beginning, returns to its origin, and draws always from that fountain which is perpetually in flood.

Bernard of Clairvaux

LOVE'S SOURCE

Sometimes I make my life so difficult. I analyze and agonize and search for some deep theological or psychological solution. But in the end, Lord, the answer is always the same: love.

The most difficult problem, the most painful family dilemmas, somehow work themselves out when I allow Your love to flow through me, like a flood of life-giving water.

Winter

During winter, the creeks and river turn icy and freeze. Snow covers the world with a frozen purity, and icicles hang from our eaves. Water is still just as present in the world, but its form has been changed by cold; caught up in the responsibilities of work and school, my family and I sometimes forget that water, even frozen, still is the source of life.

Stagnant water loses its purity and in cold water becomes frozen.

Leonardo da Vinci

FROZEN PUDDLES

When the rain fell last month, it left clear sparkling puddles in our driveway. I looked out the kitchen window and saw the sky reflected in them, turning them into blue and white pools spattered across the blacktop. But now those same puddles have grown muddy and dull. Last night's cold froze them solid.

God, my heart feels just as muddy, just as frozen. I need Your love to thaw it, I need Your grace to fill it anew. Only then will my life once again reflect eternity's bright skies.

More things
are wrought by prayer
Than this world dreams of.
Wherefore, let thy voice
Rise like a fountain
for me night and day.

Alfred Lord Tennyson

PRAYER

Outside, Lord, the world is cold and icy. When I walk down by the creek, I find it frozen solid.

But inside my heart, God, prayer leaps and dances like a fountain that shoots up toward the sky. No matter how bitter the world's cold, prayer unites me to Your warm living waters.

MOONLIGHT ON WATER

At my feet the lake is cold and dark and smooth. I can hardly believe that this is the same place that brims with life on summer days, filled then with quacking ducks and the ripple of fish, the dip and splash of canoe oars and the laughter of children. Tonight the lake lies in chilly silence. And my own heart is cold and silent too. I don't know how to pray.

And then to my surprise, the moon rises, so silently, so gradually, I barely notice until it spills its light across the dark water in a long silver trail. The lake did nothing to work this magic; it simply waited, silent and patient.

Well, Lord, here I am. Silent, dark, waiting for Your light.

Lo! the level lake
And the long glories
of the winter moon.

Alfred Lord Tennyson

Come, thou Fount of every blessing
Tune my heart to sing thy grace;
Streams of mercy never ceasing,
Call for songs of loudest praise. . . .

Prone to wander, Lord, I feel it,
Prone to leave the God I love;
Take my heart, O take and seal it,
Seal it for thy courts above.

Robert Robinson

(1735–1790)

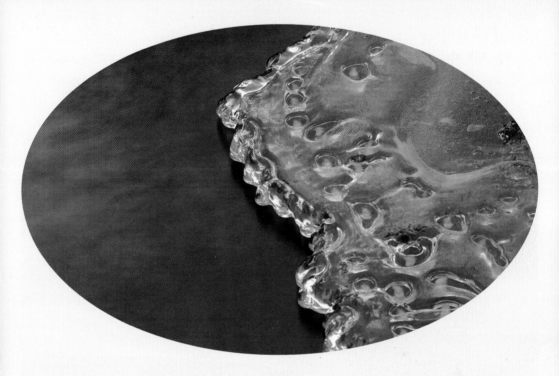

A NEVER-ENDING STREAM OF MERCY

Lord, I never seem to learn. Sooner or later, I always wander off into the desert. I know that You use my desert experiences; I know that sometimes You even lead me there, so that I will depend only on Your grace. But other times, like now, I realize I've chosen the desert needlessly, of my own volition, when You wanted only to bless me.

When my own stubborn selfishness chooses dusty death instead of life, thank You, God, that Your mercy for me still flows unchecked, a never-ending stream.

Like cold water to a weary soul,
is good news from a distant land.

Proverbs 25:25

GOOD NEWS

You know, Lord, how worried I have been for my friend who moved away. But today she called with such wonderful news! My heart is refreshed. Thank You for the cold clear water You pour into our thirsty lives. Thank You for answering prayer.

THE INVISIBLE WORLD

Lord, I've been walking along thinking what I would do if we get this salary raise. The snow has been falling around me, dropping silently into the dark river, but I've barely noticed; my thoughts are preoccupied with visions of a new car, payed-off bills, maybe even a new house. . . .

God, I want so many material things. But from Your point of view, heaven's perspective, all these visible things disappear so quickly. Like the snowflakes, they're lovely while they last, but they're gone as soon as they drop into eternity's great river.

Help me, Lord, not to be preoccupied with the fleeting things of this visible world. Fix my attention instead on the invisible world that lasts forever.

*Like the snow falls in the river—
A moment white, then melts forever.*

Robert Burns
(1759–1796)

TRUST

When the winter storms
sweep over the sea,
threatening to capsize my
little craft, remind me,
Lord, that even though I do
not always hear Your voice, You
are sleeping in my ship.

Without warning,

a furious storm came up on the lake,

so that the waves swept over the boat.

But Jesus was sleeping.

Matthew 8:24

Strike the rock, and water will come

out of it for the people to drink.

Exodus 17:6

WATER FROM THE ROCK

Right now, God, my family's life seems frozen solid. Cabin-bound by the winter storms, we're starting to get on each other's nerves. I've exhausted all my creativity and patience for keeping everyone entertained and fed and peaceful. I have to confess my voice has been louder and angrier than the children's. At the moment, I'm hiding in the bathroom; I may scream if anyone interrupts me.

But sitting here on the edge of the bathtub, I've been thinking of the Israelites. They probably got pretty sick of each other sometimes during their long, long journey. Moses must have been at his wit's end at times. And when people came to him complaining that they were thirsty, there was no lovely pool or riverbank or beach in sight, just hard, dry stones. Yet all Moses had to do was turn to You—and You brought forth water from the rock.

Well, Lord, I've exhausted my own water supplies. My heart is stony and cold. . .but I'm counting on Your grace. And even now, I feel it streaming from the rock, watering us all.

WASHING DAY

Jesus, I'm trying to imagine the scene when You washed the disciples' feet. I've always found it a little embarrassing to think about You wrapped in a towel, bent over a bunch of dirty smelly feet, washing each one gently in a pan of water. It just doesn't seem appropriate to picture the Lord of heaven doing something so everyday, so intimate, so grubby.

My Lord, after an ordinary day, my heart is soiled with the grime of selfishness. I hate to let anyone get close to me for fear they'll catch a whiff of the stale, foul smell of self. Jesus, pour Your clean water into the pan. Get out Your towel. Wash me clean.

After that, he poured water into a basin and began to wash his disciples' feet, drying them with the towel that was wrapped around him.

John 13:5

At the bottom of grace's holy river,
we see the glory of God.
We are healed, made whole,
and kept safe by grace,
through the redemption that comes from Christ,
to the praise and glory of God.
This river bottom is good and solid,
for grace will not fail.

John Bunyan

BENEATH THE ICE

As I walk through the snow beside the frozen creek, the world is silent and white. All signs of life are sleeping, covered with ice. And then, standing here with the wind sharp against my face, I hear a tiny, faraway sound: the trickle of water flowing beneath the ice.

Thank You, Lord, that no cold is so sharp that it can stop Your life at work in mine. Beneath the thickest ice this world can offer, Your glory flows on, steady and reliable, unchecked by winter's cold.

DEEP LOVE

When I hear You asking me to surrender my life to You, Lord, sometimes I stiffen up, as afraid as I was when I was a kid trying to learn to swim. I could never quite believe that the water would hold me up if I would simply relax and trust.

But You're not asking for a one-sided arrangement here, one where I give up everything while You remain distant and unmoving. No, You, Jesus, have already surrendered Yourself to me. In those long-ago swimming lessons, I was already enveloped in water's buoyancy, and in the same way, I am surrounded today with all You have given me—so what can I do but trust You to bear me up in the deep current of Your love?

O the deep, deep love of Jesus,

Vast, unmeasured, boundless, free;

Rolling as a mighty ocean

In its fullness over me.

Underneath me, all around me,

Is the current of thy love.

Samuel Trevor Francis
(1834–1925)

Old winter's frost and hoary hair
With garlands crowned. . .
The nipping frost of wrath is gone,
To Him the manger made a throne.
Due praises let us sing,
Winter and spring.

Thomas Traherne
(1637–1674), "On Christmas Day"

SPRING IN THE MIDST OF WINTER

The whole earth lies white and sleeping; everything looks dead and cold. The lake is a smooth solid sheet, the creek is silent now, and the river's life is deep beneath a layer of ice. Nothing grows in all this cold.

And yet we defy winter, and hang our house with evergreen. Christmas comes not when the world is wet and green and brimming with life. No, dear Lord, today, one of the coldest, shortest days of all the year, marks Your birth into our world.

JOY!

The hills and fields outside my window are hushed and frozen, each tiny twig and dry blade of grass hung with a bead of ice. Water hangs suspended, frozen from every surface, its fluid, life-giving power turned solid and dormant.

And then the rising sun makes this cold world gleam, turning everything to diamond-fire, a world decorated to receive its King. Let me never forget, Lord, that the joy of Your birth sings everywhere today, even in our cold, wintry hearts.

Joy to the world! the Savior reigns;
Let men their songs employ,
While fields and floods, rocks, hills, and plains,
Repeat the sounding joy.

Isaac Watts
(1674–1748)

I have come into the deep waters; the floods engulf me.

Psalm 69:2

FLOOD WATERS

I know that water gives us life, Lord. But surely this is too much of a good thing? This sudden winter thaw has turned two feet of snow into torrents of water pouring off the hillsides, into the river. Our little creek has turned into a roaring flood of brownish yellow that's overflowed its banks, taking out the bridge down the road and swamping our neighbors' houses. We're lucky that our basement is only flooded, and not our living room.

This isn't life-giving, Lord; this is destructive!

But I overheard a farmer talking today. He said that the soil is always richer after a flood. "Next year," he predicted, "my corn will grow taller in that flooded field."

Is it the same with Your grace, God? Sometimes I feel as though my life is drowning, swamped by life's destruction. But when the floodwaters retreat at last, will my life yield a richer harvest?

FLOOD RELIEF

The flood keeps rising higher and higher, swamping fields and lawns, washing away roads. And my husband is somewhere across the state, on his way home from a business trip. I wish he were here now, Lord, safe with me inside our home.

Everything has seemed to go wrong while he was gone. The children are sick with the chickenpox, the car has broken down, the furnace isn't working right, and the water in our basement keeps rising higher. I want my husband home—but mostly, I just want him safe. I'm scared.

But, Lord, You know where he is. He is in Your hands out there amid the flooded roads, as safe as if he were here with me. And I am safe too. When life threatens to overwhelm us, You will rescue us from the flood.

He reached down from on high and took hold of me; he drew me out of deep waters.

2 Samuel 22:17

SAFETY

God is my only source of safety. No human being can take His place, not my husband or my parents or my closest friends. Even the wind and waves listened to His voice. Why should I be afraid?

Be still, my soul:
the waves and winds still know
His voice who ruled
them while he dwelt below.
Be still, my soul:
when change and tears are past,
All safe and blessed
we shall meet at last.

Katharina von Schlegel,
b. 1693

Many waters cannot quench love; rivers cannot wash it away.

Song of Solomon 8:7

UNQUENCHABLE LOVE

Last night, my husband made it safely home at last, despite the floods. Today I rejoice in his presence, grateful for his safety and our love.

I rejoice in Your presence too, my Lord. Thank You that no matter what happens to me, no matter how deep and cold the flood, Your love is never quenched.

Spring

In spring, the frozen rivers and lakes come back to life again. Melted snow streams off the hills, and slowly, little by little, everything turns green. My family delights in being outside again—and the new life we see around us reminds us of the awesome reality of Christ's resurrection.

Cast your bread upon the waters, for after many days you will find it again.
Ecclesiastes 11:1

BREAD UPON THE WATERS

The Northeast is still in the grip of a wintry March, but our family has escaped to our favorite warm, southern beach. Today, as we threw bags of stale bread out into the waves for the gulls, I found myself thinking about that verse in Ecclesiastes. Lord, what does it mean to throw my bread upon the water?

I don't think the Scripture was promising that our old crusts would come washing up to shore again, soggy and nibbled by the birds and fish. No, I think the Bible must have meant that something unexpected, something that seems humanly irrational, something miraculous, would happen.

So, Lord, here's everything in my life that looks like bread to me, the things that nourish me: my family, my career, my home. I'm throwing the whole bag out onto the sea of Your love. Common sense warns me this is a dangerous and foolish move.

But common sense will never grasp the wonder of Your love.

And God said, "Let the water teem
with living creatures. . . ."
So God created the great creatures of the sea and every
living and moving thing with which the water
teems, according to their kinds. . . .
And God saw that it was good.
God blessed them and said, "Be fruitful, and increase
in number and fill the water in the seas. . . ."

Genesis 1:20–22

ABUNDANT BLESSINGS

Walking beside the ocean today, Lord, I am overwhelmed by the bounty of creation: twinkly sandpipers and soaring pelicans, the rolling fin of a dolphin among the waves and a tiny creature that quivers on the sand like a spoonful of transparent jelly. All this You created!

And that same creativity is at work in me, bringing forth life, making me fruitful, multiplying the bounty of gifts You have already given me. Thank You, God, for Your abundant blessings.

Many a congregation when it assembles in church
must look to the angels like a muddy,
puddly shore at low tide; littered
with every kind of rubbish and odds and ends. . . .
And then the tide of worship comes in, and it's all gone:
the dead sea urchins and jelly-fish, the paper,
and the empty cans and the nameless bits of rubbish.
The cleansing sea flows over the whole lot.
So we are released from a narrow,
selfish outlook on the universe
by a common act of worship.

Evelyn Underhill

A TIDE OF WORSHIP

At low tide, my children and I clean up the beach. We collect bags of garbage, old soda cans and potato chip wrappers and broken sand buckets. I think to myself that it's an endless, hopeless job, but my children never give up. And then the tide comes in, wiping the cluttered beach clean, filling it with tossing, sparkling waves.

Sometimes at church, Lord, all I can see are the human flaws and failures that clutter up our congregation. You call us to be Your Body here on earth—but working toward that perfect unity is a never-ending and thankless job. I have to admit that all too often I feel resentful and frustrated when people don't meet my standards.

And then on Sunday morning, I hear our voices lifted together as we sing "Amazing Grace"—and as we lay aside our differences and join in praise, our all too-human congregation is washed clean in the shining tide of worship.

The fall of dripping water hollows the stone.

Lucretius (99-55 B.C.)

DRIPPING WATER

Sometimes, Jesus, I feel as though I'll never change. Walking along the creek today, I saw new life bursting from every twig and clump of earth. Just as spring is transforming the earth, I want to be transformed, too. I long for Your new life to burst out of me, as sudden and spectacular as fireworks. Instead, again and again I fall into the same old selfish habits.

And then lying on the ground I noticed a stone shaped like a shallow cup. *Did I shape this stone with dynamite?* I seemed to hear You whisper. *Or did I take a thousand years and countless tiny drips of water to change its form?*

Oh Jesus, wear away my selfishness, so my heart can cup Your living water. Help me to be patient while Your grace flows drop by drop into my life.

90

As the rain and the snow come down from heaven,
and do not return to it without watering the earth
and making it bud and flourish. . .
so is my word that goes out from my mouth.

Isaiah 55:10–11

NEW LIFE

The creeks and rivers are full of fast, bright water, and everywhere I look I see the earth coming back to life. After our long, stormy winter, the sun is shining again. The hills are suddenly clothed with green.

And as I look back at this year, Lord, I see now that even in the storms You were sending Your word into my heart. And now at last I feel myself begin to grow, bursting forth into new life.

Because water

is transparent,

it can receive light;

and so

it is fitting

that it should

be used

in baptism,

inasmuch as it is

the sacrament

of faith.

Thomas Aquinas

BAPTISM WATER

This past winter, the heavy snows and floods were frightening and destructive. The earth was buried in snow, drowned in icy water. . .and yet now, with the spring, the earth is resurrected, brought back to new, green life.

Lord, in baptism my old self was destroyed, submerged beneath the water. But You did not leave me water-logged and dying. By faith, I live again. The same water that killed my old sinful identity now fills me with light and life.

I will make rivers flow on barren heights. . . I will put in the desert the cedar and the acacia, the myrtle and the olive. I will set pines in the wasteland, the fir and the cypress together.

Isaiah 41:18–19

ROOTED IN CHRIST

I'm all alone today except for the trees that grow beside me on the bank. The young leaves of sycamores and locust trees and willows look like green lace against the bright sky. Each tree's leaves are different from the others, but all their roots draw life from the creek's water.

Lately, Jesus, I've been noticing how different the members of Your Body are from one another. One is fiery and dogmatic, another gentle and soft-spoken; one carries his faith like a soldier's banner, while another lives a life of quiet love. Sometimes I'm drawn to one person, sometimes another individual irritates me.

Remind me, Lord, that we are each beautiful in Your sight. You long to bless us all. And let us never forget that we draw our life from one common Source.

We have a God who wants to bless a multiplicity of people in a multiplicity of ways. . . . He says. . . , "Each of you is uniquely beautiful, but you have this in common: you all need water at your roots."

Luci Shaw

The Touch of Eternity

Lord, sitting beside this tiny blue lake I find myself thinking not of the picnic I should be packing or even of the ducks that paddle around me, hoping for bread, but of something far bigger and far less concrete: eternity.

My children are missing Grandpa Jack. "He's in heaven now," I promise them, and I know I speak the truth. But at the same time, doubt comes creeping up to nibble at my mind: What if heaven is just a pretty story we've told ourselves, a dream too good to be true?

And then I hear You say, "In My Father's house are many mansions. If this weren't so, I would have told you." If heaven is a dream, the happy ending with which we comfort ourselves, then it is a dream come true, and the story is the truest one ever told—because You are the one who told it to us.

In front of me, the lake is the same color as the sky above. It's only a reflection, of course—but it's an accurate reflection, nonetheless, for the sky above my head is a deep, true blue. And as I look out at the water, I realize that the lake is not reflecting something distant and remote. No, the sky meets the water, just as eternity touches my own heart.

Let them dream life just as the lake dreams the sky.

Miguel de Unamuno

Water is the secret of green. . . .
It means hope and health
where there would otherwise be
only despair and death.

Luci Shaw,
Water My Soul

DEPENDENT ON GRACE

Our new garden cannot grow with water. Without Your grace, Lord, neither can I.

Drop thy still dews of quietness,
Till all our striving cease. . .
And let our ordered lives confess
The beauty of thy peace.

John Greenleaf Whittier
(1807–1892)

GOD'S DEW

My children have gotten used to finding the lawn crisp with frost when they go out to meet the school bus. Today, though, the air is warmer, and every blade of grass, every new leaf, glistens with drops of dew. My youngest daughter is enchanted to find "diamonds" hanging from her favorite tree. "What makes them?" she asks.

Her scientific older brother is happy to explain condensation to her: "When the wet warm air hits the cold ground, the water falls out of the air and turns to dew."

God, thank You that wherever the warm and living Spirit touches my cold life, Your quiet peace clings to me like dew.

SUNLIT SHOWERS

When I looked out my window just now, I found that the sun was shining through the rain. The trees and grass looked as though they were being showered with liquid light.

Thank You, Lord, that Your light streams over us every moment—even in the rain.

Thy beautiful care what tongue can recite?
It breathes in the air,
it shines in the light;
It streams from the hills,
it descends to the plain,
And sweetly distills in the dew and the rain.

Sir Robert Grant
(1779–1838)

You will again have compassion on us;
You will tread our sins underfoot and hurl all our
iniquities into the depths of the sea.
Micah 7:19

THE DEPTHS OF THE SEA

God, I'm glad You didn't say You would throw my sin into the little creek that flows beside our house—or even into our favorite Adirondack lake. No, I'm afraid the water is too shallow in both those places, and sooner or later all the things I don't like about myself would come bobbing to the surface.

Instead, You have dropped my sins—all my selfishness and imperfections—to the very bottom of the ocean floor. They are gone forever beneath the fathoms. . .and I am free and perfect in Your sight.

The river's ripple calms my troubled heart today; I am reluctant to leave this green, quiet spot and go back to face my life.

I've done it again: I've lost touch with the Spirit's gentle voice within my heart, and I've forgotten to follow Christ's rule of love. And now I have to face the consequences in my life.

Well, Lord, I suppose I could sit here wallowing in my guilt all day—but that doesn't put me back in touch with Your Spirit. So I won't waste any more time; here is my heart, open to You once more. May Your river of peace flow into me, so that I can again be a channel for Your love.

If only you had paid attention to my commands, your peace would have been like a river.

Isaiah 48:18

When they walk through the Valley of Weeping,
it will become a place of refreshing springs,
where pools of blessing collect after the rains!

Psalm 84:6, NLT

POOLS OF BLESSING

Our back lawn is full of little shimmering pools of water left behind by the spring rains. As I look out at them, though, I can barely see them, for my eyes are full of tears and my heart is sore and heavy. How can our family face another crisis now? How can we endure another round of hospital visits and long worried days waiting for test results? Why couldn't our family simply enjoy the spring?

But when I blink the tears from my eyes, those small, gleaming pools outside come into focus. I take a deep breath. And then I let my fear drop into Your love, for You have taught me over and over that even in my deepest sorrow, Your rain always leaves pools of blessing in my life.

POLISHED BY GRACE

My children have a new hobby: They
paint round stones, turning them into
ladybugs and turtles and curled up,
sleeping cats. We've discovered that we
find the smoothest, roundest stones where
the river runs the fastest.

Lord, my life has been running fast
and hard these past few weeks, and I
feel tumbled and tossed. But I'm trust-
ing You. Wear away my sharp edges.
May my heart be smooth and polished by
Your grace.

Let the rivers clap their hands. . . .

Psalm 98:8

SONG!

Lord, thank You for the good news we had today! You gave us peace even in our trouble—but now that peace has taken wings, for Your mercy has triumphed over sickness. I feel as though I might fly away.

Since I'm short on physical wings, though, our family celebrates instead on the riverbank, eating tuna fish sandwiches and homemade chocolate chip cookies. As I lay out the feast, the children play in water that has been warmed by days of sunshine. The thick green leaves above our heads carry the promise of summer, and I find myself humming the hymn, "Like a River Glorious."

I remember a story about this hymn's author, Frances Ridley Havergal. In the midst of her own personal crisis, she wrote, "Now 'Thy will be done' is not a sigh, but only a song!"

As I sit here on the riverbank, mere prayer is not enough. I must sing!

Like a river glorious
Is God's perfect peace
Over all victorious
In its bright increase.

Frances Ridley Havergal

(1836–1878)

*Its roots
may grow old
in the ground
and its stump
die in the soil,
yet at the scent
of water
it will bud
and put forth shoots
like a plant.*

Job 14:8–9

I feel so old lately, God. My grown-up responsibilities pile up, and I feel tired and worn down, like an old stump that has lost all its lovely branches. Some days I just don't have time for joy; I'm just too tired to laugh.

And then the spring wind blows in from the south, carrying the scent of rain. I take a breath—and my dry wood bursts into buds of life. Suddenly, anything seems possible!

Give me a child's heart again, Lord, one that leaps up in life and laughter. Remind me that the breath of Your Spirit always brings the promise of Living Water. May the scent of that water keep spring alive in me throughout eternity.

THE CYCLE OF SEASONS

As summer comes once more, my children complete the school year, marking a new milestone in their lives. As we begin another year's cycle, we will face a whole new set of joys and sorrows. We will have days of sunshine by the sea—and we will face cold storms that shake our lives. We will send our roots down deep into God's Living Water, growing strong and green—and we will endure long, arid droughts. But through all the changing seasons of our lives, God's promise is clear: We will never escape God's Spirit. If we go down to the place of the dead, He is there; if we ride the wings of the morning, if we dwell by the farthest oceans, even there His hand will guide us and His strength will support us (Psalm 139:7, 9–10, paraphrased).

A boundless vision
grows upon us. . .
river, lake,
and glimmering pool;
wilderness oceans mingling
with the sky.
Francis Parkman (1823–1893)

ORDINARY REVELATIONS

In a glass of clear water, in a noisy creek, in calm lakes, and in stormy seas, God, I have caught Your reflection. Thank You for giving Yourself to me over and over, day after day, instant by instant. I am grateful for all the quiet times beside the water when You never failed to run out to greet my praying heart. Each season of this year, in a hundred ordinary, everyday moments, You helped me glimpse eternity.

Like water spilled on the ground,

which cannot be recovered,

so we must die.

But God does not take away life;

instead, he devises ways

so that a banished person

may not remain

estranged from him.

2 Samuel 14:14

SPILL-PROOF

If I spill a glass of water on the ground, there's no point trying to pick the water up again; it's gone. But I'm glad that when we die, we will not disappear, like spilled water soaked up by the earth. Thanks to You, Jesus, we will never be banished from Your life-giving presence. The Water of Life can't be spilled—and it never evaporates.

. . . like aloes planted by the LORD. . . . Water will flow from their buckets; their seed will have abundant water.

Numbers 24:6–7

SHARING THE WATER

An aloe's thick leaves store the water it sucks up through its roots—and then somehow, within the leaves, that moisture is transformed into a soothing lotion. That's why my mother keeps an aloe plant on her kitchen window sill; if any of us burn ourselves cooking, she can quickly pinch off a succulent leaf and squeeze the healing sap onto the burn. Lord, make me like an aloe plant. Remind me that when You water me with Your grace, You want me to pass Your love onto others. May Your Living Water be always present in me, so that peace and health will flow from me to those in need.

CONCLUSION

God is beyond all our human capabilities of comprehension. He is simply too big for us to grasp. That's why we need to use images and metaphors: They help us touch the eternal world, the world our earthly fingers are too insensitive to feel. These symbols allow us to stand on tiptoe and peek into God's kingdom.

Water is one of our most powerful images for God's grace. The Bible has around a thousand references to water and bodies of water, and as we read the Scriptures, we gain a sense of God's love and grace flowing steadily through the text, like a clean, life-giving stream.

May we also, then, whenever we see a river reflect the sunlight, whenever we walk along an ocean beach, whenever we hear the rain patter against our windows, remember to turn our hearts toward the One who is our Living Water: Jesus Christ. This world gives us only faint glimpses of eternity's beauty; as Paul said in his first letter to the Corinthians,

"Now we see but a poor reflection.
But one day, we will see face to face,
and then we will know fully."

We will drink deep of the real water, the Living Water, and we will never be thirsty again.